# Acting With Honor
# And As King

## By: Trent Goodbaudy

Copyright © 2013 Trent Goodbaudy

Published in Portland, Oregon by PDXdzyn. PDXdzyn is a trademark of Trent Goodbaudy. PDXdzyn titles may be purchased in bulk for educational, business, fund-raising, or sales promotional use. For information, please send email to info@pdxdzyn.com.

Also visit: FREEDOM*from*GOVERNMENT.US

and shop.TrentGoodbaudy.com

*Printed in the United States of America.*

ISBN-13: **978-1492192930**
ISBN-10: **1492192937**

BISAC Category: Education / Teaching Methods & Materials / Arts & Humanities

## DEDICATION

For all of the Private Peaceful Inhabitants of Planet Earth.

# FREEDOM *from* GOVERNMENT
## Acting With Honor and As King

# Contents:

Introduction

1 .................. Who is the Problem - 6

2 ................................. Fear - 10

3 ........................... Argument - 12

4 .............. Honor and Controversy - 14

5 .........................What do you own? - 15

6 ............................ The Name - 17

7 ............................. As-King - 21

Conclusion

# INTRODUCTION

This book is a quick read. I did that on purpose. It is to get you caught up to speed as absolutely quick as possible. We don't have any time to mess around; we have to start taking back what is ours, today.

This book is about how to deal with any law enforcement, lawyers, judges, clerks, bailiffs, and ANY other type of individual that you interact with that is trying to cause you harm. Without knowing how to file or fill out paperwork, without knowing or even having to care about court procedure laws or statutes or policy and it doesn't matter WHERE you are in the WORLD!

This is finally YOUR silver bullet that THEY said didn't exist.

I wish I could have had this information 30 years ago. My entire life would have been different.

Once you understand the concepts in this book, and your words, demeanor, and actions come from the heart, you will be surrounded with an impenetrable shield of love so strong that nothing can break through.

It isn't that you will be untouchable, you will instead be protected. Whoever you come in contact with in any aspect of your life, when you stay in honor you will feel a warmth within and have a radiant outer glow about you.

People will not usually even be able to identify how you are doing it, but it will serve you well if you understand and practice the concepts within these pages to become a private peaceful inhabitant.

It is not about getting away with anything, it is about being left alone to live in peace.

# Who is the Problem?

You already know the material in this book. It is knowledge that everyone is born with.

There is a problem however, and this problem is that it really has nothing to do with anyone but you. No one can change you BUT you. Don't worry about anyone else. This book is all about you, and claiming your true power as your own king in your life. Don't lose focus of the goal. This book is not about anyone else or any other exterior problems you may be having while you read this book.

Take a break from them for now, and allow your troubles the chance to work themselves out after you have done the inner work you need to do for yourself.

In times long past and sometimes even today the title *master* was retained and used for boys or young men.

Why do you think this is? Is it because as a child, your thoughts and actions are more pure and uncorrupted by the world around you? Maybe it is because children ask lots of questions. Or perhaps, just living in this world for a period of time is what corrupts the souls of men. No matter what happened, it is time to once again look at the world as a child without all the preconceived notions that are held by adults.

A child is inquisitive, and is looking for answers. They inquire about everything. Let this be your first clue, to be successful in not only interaction with agents of government, but in just about every aspect of your life.

The secret is to inquire.

But what happens as you grow older? You start becoming more self-conscious and start caring about what other people think about you. You want to sound smart, so you slow down or stop asking questions completely and just act like you know the answers. This is where the problem begins: with belief.

Belief is a problem because it allows a concept take hold in the mind that is usually accepted without real investigation. If no one was gullible and everyone challenged every belief that didn't have merit, people would be tricked much less and I think the world would be a beautiful place if this mixed with individual responsibility and morality (which is simply knowing the difference between right and wrong).

Have you ever met someone that knows everything? Or thinks that they do, but when you present a new idea they will say they already knew that? Or maybe not tell you, or ask any questions if they don't know something? Or act like they already knew something when you expand their knowledge with a new tid-bit?

This person is done asking questions. They have inhibited their own expansion of knowledge because they don't want look or sound stupid. Sounds really contradictory doesn't it?

These people might think that it is better to *act stupid*, instead of just *sounding stupid*.

This is just how the human mind works, to overcome it and defeat it you only have to recognize it and work to be more open.

People are lost when it comes to dealing with court and police, and I believe it is just because they don't know what to do; and people would know what to do, if only they knew who they are.

People don't want to learn what to do about these situations, or ever challenge the presumed authority of these agents because they carry weapons and they take people's freedom away. Sometimes they even seriously injure or kill people. You don't want to tell them that they are wrong.

A smart person will learn from what they do wrong, it is called gaining experience. You don't learn anything by never trying, so trying is how you actually learn. Why do you do the same thing every day? Why does everything seem so structured?

Ask questions, and be open to interaction with others, and keep an open mind. You could wake up one day and realize everything you have been told is a lie.

You were born free... right?

Do you still feel as free as the day you were born? I guess you probably can't remember the day you were born, but what has happened to your freedom since? Is it external sources that are preventing you from being free, or is it your own mind? What is really preventing you from being as free as you would like to be right now?

Is it the corrupt courts? The police? Your job? Your spouse? Your kids? The guy on the freeway on-ramp with a sign that is asking for spare change? Stupid drivers? Stupid people? Or maybe it is the fact that you are looking for someone or something to blame. You have nothing and no one to blame at all, and once you realize this and actually stop blaming external things that are out of your control, you will move forward.

There is no blame needed. All that is needed is determination, persistence and an open mind.

When you are in court, and you answer their questions with statements, you are actually testifying against yourself. So in that case, who would be committing the fraud? The court? The court is just asking questions. You are the one making the statements. If they ask you a question and you answer it, what does that make you?

Have you ever heard the saying: "the master asks the questions and the servant answers them"? The minute you answer that question, you have just given them jurisdiction.

You are the one that testifies against yourself. You are the one committing fraud. Ignorance is no excuse, now that you have been informed.

What happens if you don't testify against yourself? My guess is that they would have to let you go.

# Fear

Guns, handcuffs, tasers, clubs, pepper spray, jail, fines, injury, and even death are very valid things to be afraid of. All of these things you're afraid of though rely on the actions of others.

There's no reason to be scared of a gun without somebody pulling trigger. There's no reason to be scared of handcuffs without someone putting them on you. There's no reason to be scared of a club if no one is swinging one. There's no reason to be scared of jail without someone there to lock you up.

What is the common denominator in all of these things that you're scared of? They all require the actions of other people.

We must realize that all we have to do is interact properly with other people and as a result, you will have no reason to be scared of any of these things. Your fear belongs to you and you alone.

So am *I* scared of these things? And the people that use them? And what they could possibly do to me?

Of course I am, but I don't let that be reflected in my interaction with them.

Ever.

Let me tell you little secret; no matter what happens to me during *the* life I am living, letting fear dictate my actions will corrupt the results.

Just like fearing death, there is no reason to because it happens to everyone, and there's no way to predict when it will happen to you. If you let it though, you could probably worry about death to the point that you couldn't function, but what good would that do? So why let fear dictate your actions, if you can't predict the future?

**Live in the moment**; do not allow the future or the past to control what you do right now.

No one can predict when the grim reaper is going to come knocking, so all you can do is live in the now, and **ENJOY IT!**

You only have one opportunity to live this life.

Something as simple as the sound of police radio static or handcuffs clicking can trigger a response (you are going to jail), and trick you into responding in such a way to bring you into their jurisdiction.

Like touching a hot stove, you immediately react. Maybe you have heard of Pavlov's dogs that were trained to salivate at the sound of a bell. You have to recognize these tactics and not let them affect you. They will do whatever they can to try and change your mind.

The attorneys, police, and judges are allowed to say things. They are allowed to lie to you, but these tactics are just to get you to play. Keep in mind that they will usually not carry through with their threats, especially if you stay in honor.

No one wants to go to jail, get shot or beat up, so they have a pretty heavy control mechanism in place. You can be sure that they have studied mind control and psychology in serious depth.

Look at their resources; they have plenty of money that they have tricked everyone into giving them. To think that they have not mastered controlling the human mind is naïve. Learn about mind control.

Once you see that it is there, it will no longer be able to affect you.

Keep in mind too that your thoughts create your reality. Watch what you think, you might just get (or create) what you are dwelling on. Make your thoughts happy, and re-channel your fear into courage.

It is okay to have fear. Sometimes fear of death keeps us alive and even helps us to do things that we would normally never be able to do. But to let fear control you, is to be out of control.

# Argument

"I am not going to argue with you!" is a common response from police officers when you try to talk them. It is an easy way for them to close down the conversation.

You never want to argue, because to argue is to get stuck in a form of a duel. You can and probably will lose.

In law school, typically for the final exam students will be chosen to represent a side in a historic case with a landmark decision.

Each side will argue, and the best argument will win. But anyone can win; all you have to do is have the best argument.

Lawyers are bound to procedure. They are unable to challenge the court because they have sworn an oath to uphold its rules.

All they can do is argue, they cannot question procedure because it is a rule. And once you've sworn an oath to uphold something, it is binding on your soul. Oaths are bad because once you swear them; you lose the ability to make certain choices in the future.

We never want to argue. And to do this, we may need to relearn how to think. Let's think about an argument for second.

What is an argument? Wikipedia says: *"In **logic** and **philosophy**, an **argument** is an attempt to persuade someone of something, by giving reasons for accepting a particular conclusion as evident. The general structure of an argument in a **natural language** is that of premises (typically in the form of **propositions**, **statements** or **sentences**) in support of a **claim**: the conclusion. The structure of some arguments can also be set out in a **formal language**, and formally-defined "arguments" can be made independently of natural language arguments, as in math, logic and computer science."*

So an argument is an attempt to persuade someone of something in support of a *claim*. It is *only* an attempt; we need something better than that. Not only can an attempt fail, but the word "attempt" doesn't sound like it could even be very effective in the first place. We're not trying to persuade anyone of anything, it is not necessary. An argument is constructed of propositions, statements and sentences. An argument is not final, and typically, an argument can be disproven, rebutted or compromised.

# Honor and Controversy

If you treat someone with honor and respect, what can you expect in return?

If you get stopped by an officer and you start screaming: "I know my rights!"

The officer is going to say to himself: "Really, you know your rights... huh, well I am going to show you what your rights are!"

And then you're in a world of crap, because you have to sue, fight your way through court, deal with jail, maybe even an ass kicking, and altogether not have a good time.

In the end, you are at *war* instead of being honorable.

A police officer is just a man. Like you. If you treat him with kindness and honor, how do you think he will treat you?

Are you trying to get out of something? If you have done harm to another's body or property, you need to take responsibility and do what you can to make it right, but that doesn't mean you need to enter a guilty plea.

What does it mean to be guilty anyway? Does it mean you really feel bad? Or is it like calling a truce because you got caught doing something against the "law", without feeling any genuine guilt?

**ALWAYS** be honorable! **TO** be honorable is to **NOT** cause controversy. You cause a **CONTROVERSY** when you claim something you do not own (namely... *THE* name). Always call it "**the name**"... for your own safety. It's "the name that you use."

Easy as that, and remember that you ARE not a fictional entity whose only existence is on a piece of paper. And if someone is mistaking you the Man or Woman for a piece of paper, there has obviously been a mistake.

So what is that mistake? *"WHO* am I to say what the mistake is... *WHO AM I???"* (the mistake is in *WHO* I actually am)

# What do you own?

Do you own your possessions or just have right-of-use?

I hate to break it to you, but you probably don't own anything. Although possession is 9/10ths of the law, all of your big purchases are all registered, deeded, or certified.

Do you know what that means? It means that all of your possessions that you worked hardest to get are probably really not even yours.

Take your house for example, do you have a deed? Does the deed itself refer to the inhabitant or owner as a "tenant"? I think it probably does. Does the title for your car say "Title" on it? Or does it say "Certificate of Title"? Do you know what the difference between the two is?

How about YOU? Do you OWN you? Are you sure? How do you know? Do you have evidence to prove it? I would not be claiming things that I don't have evidence of ownership of.

And if you have a "Birth Certificate"... guess what that means? It means that your birth was certified by the government. Guess what else? If your birth was certified by government, it means that they own your name. Unless and until you rescind, or use a process to demand back or nullify the registration of the birth.

The good news is that you did not have the mental facilities to enter into a contract when you were born. This means that "full disclosure" would have been impossible, and any contracts or agreements made without full disclosure are fraudulent, and all fraudulent contracts are void ab initio. Or invalid on their face, from the beginning.

But not until you have noticed and defaulted the government on the issue and completed the process to remedy the birth certificate controversy, you cannot claim ownership over their certified security, which you know as your name. It isn't your name, it just *sounds like* your name.

But it isn't YOUR name… yet anyway (right?), most likely, so you cannot claim it without causing controversy as far as the court and police are concerned.

# The Name

Who are you? Are you your name? What is your name? I was not asking for your name in the previous question, I was asking if you know what your name actually is, or represents.

Not only is it what people call you when they want to get your attention, but it is something that was "given" to you when you were born.

Do you know the difference between your "family" name, and your "given" name?

Your "given" name is actually a legal fiction because it is not "part" of you; it was "given" to you, like a gift. And as soon as your birth was certified, it actually became a corporate entity.

The "family" name is the one handed down by the father, and it is actually considered to be part of you, as your father's seed physically created the embryo. I was looking at my birth certificate the other day, and there was a space for my mother's signature, but no place for my dad's signature at all.

Can you guess why there was no space for his signature on the birth certificate?

Well, I have had police use asking about the "given" name as a way to gain subject matter jurisdiction. How else would they be able to do it? It wouldn't be your family name that they are using to gain jurisdiction, because it is always about the "name" your mother gave you.

Please don't ever admit to government that you are your given name... if for no other reason than you cannot be a name, because a name is made of letters... not skin, bones, blood, organs and a soul.

Everything you should know should be based on your own first-hand experience. I cannot really claim anything to be fact unless it manifests in the physical world. It is hard to differentiate in a world of fictions, but facts are always self-evident or easily demonstrated.

You don't need to know anything about the court rules, procedure, customs, or even location. It is so simple. It is your name. What if the whole time you were in court, you didn't claim the name? If you can stay away from the name, there is nothing that they can do to you. It is so simple. Why would you need to know anything about any laws? You can find out what you need to know by asking questions.

**The first (and most important) element of jurisdiction:** "*The accused must be properly identified; identified in such a fashion there is no room for mistaken identity. The individual must be singled out from all others; otherwise, anyone could be subject to arrest and trial without benefit of "wrong party" defense. Almost always the means of identification is a person's proper name, BUT, any means of identification is equally valid if said means differentiates the accused without doubt. (By the way, there is no constitutionally valid requirement that you must identify yourself to the judge or to anyone.) For stop and identify issues (4th Amendment) see Brown v. Texas, 443 US 47 and Kolender v Lawson, 461 US 352.*

Police can also gain subject matter jurisdiction simply by asking "is this your car?" You might be wondering how… well because the registered owner is your "given" name or fictional legal "person". And once again, by claiming to own the name (via claiming ownership of the car that you likely don't really own either), you cause a controversy and go out of honor.

A judge might even throw you in jail as a test just to see if you claim the name. **Don't do it.**

If they get past the issue of the name, they presume to have jurisdiction on you. If this ever happens, you say *"I think that there has been a mistake, if anybody here has been upset or offended by anything I may have said or done, can I be forgiven? I ask that you please forgive me."*

If you say *"I'm sorry"*… you are guilty. **ALWAYS** phrase your response in the form of a question.

So how does one get past the "What is your name?" question?

Well, if your name is something you have right-of-use of, but not ownership of, wouldn't it be something that you "use" like a spoon, or a fork, or a television?

Always refer to the name as *"the"* name, never my name, or I am… You have to be very careful to not ever let the legal nexus be made or connect the fictitious government owned given name with the real flesh and blood family name.

It is **THE** name that you **USE**. It is not yours, although people call you something that sounds very similar, they are not talking about that name in court. They are ALWAYS talking about the name "given" to the corporate entity.

# As-King

How does a king act? He acts with honor. He tells the truth. He does not commit fraud. He knows to ask questions, and you usually can't quite tell what it is about him, but he commands respect. When you begin to act as a king, you will be doing the as-king.

You can either spend your time and spin your gears trying to make people pay for the wrongs they did to you, or you can find out how they legitimized their actions to begin with, and nip it as soon as possible when dealing with them.

Public officials have strict procedure that they must follow. Asking questions and using non-rebuttables really puts a kink in their procedure. You see, they need to get you to testify against yourself, and if you never give them any information, they won't be able to follow procedure. They will probably call a supervisor, and try again to get you to admit to being the name with all kinds of tricks, but don't fall for it. If you do it right, the chances that they will just leave you alone are 99.9%.

If you deal with them in question form, the chances are that they will just go away. Guess, what? This works with just about any kind of interaction in your life. Bullies, security guards, bouncers, bill collectors, attorneys, judges, probation officers, even bums on the street, and trolls on the internet! So once you get some practice, you will be absolutely unstoppable.

Try it starting today, just ask questions.

It is like a tennis game. The ball goes back and forth; whoever misses the ball loses the point. Keep the ball in the air. Like when Neo avoids the bullets for the first time in the Matrix, and Trinity asks "How did you do that? You moved just like they did!" And Neo says that he obviously didn't move fast enough, because he got grazed by one of the bullets.

If the judge is blasting you with questions, you have to move like they do and come right back with more questions.
It is easy to get sidetracked. The judge will ask a bunch of real simple questions to try and get you to slip up. You have to stay on your toes, and be quick on your feet to keep up.

They will put on the pressure and distract you with something like "I am about to charge you with contempt", and then ask a quick question like "How old are you?" with a simple answer that you are likely in the habit of just rattling off a number to try and get you to into their jurisdiction. Or the judge may ask something like "Where were you born?", and you might ask if it is required to for me to answer that question, and the judge could reply with "That's your answer?!?!" just to try and throw you off.

Do not ever answer "yes" or "no"!

If you ever get caught up in that kind of trap and you find that they have moved from the "name" to other matters, it is time to ask if you have made a mistake and you would like to please be forgiven.

Keep in mind too that you don't have to answer immediately; you can always take a second or two and take a deep breath, and think of a good question to respond with. So just because the judge is on rapid-fire doesn't mean you have to answer as fast as the shells are being fired at you.

Judges and lawyers are taught to deflect also, usually answering with a non-answer or question. They will sound like they are answering a question, but they are really just throwing you a curve ball. For example, when you ask a question like "Would you agree that I am not required to testify against myself?" They will deflect with something like "Everyone has that right." Instead of answering the question as it pertains to your situation individually.

You can do all the preparation you want, but there is no substitute for actual experience under pressure with your freedom on the line.

When you get in there, it becomes very real and you forget everything. But when you have finally opened that door and faced that fear, you are going to be introduced into another world.

You will see a world that you have never seen before, because the fear always stopped you. The fear keeps you blind, but once you lose the fear there are great rewards that come with your new world.

You might not get it on the first try, but keep working at it and you will learn from your mistakes and get better. With the fear gone, none of it will be real anymore. It will be like at the end of the first Matrix movie, when Neo stops the bullets and sees the green strings of code that the matrix is made up of. Not real.

UN-real.

And make sure that If you do end up going to jail, use it as a learning experience and respond as-king while you are there. And you won't be there for long anyway, plus the jail staff will love you even more for practicing on them.

If you do it right, they have to give you a way out. If you pass all the tests, do you think they are going to keep testing you?

Of course they are going to throw everything they've got at you, but once you know how to ask the appropriate questions, it will all be ineffective. Judges are not bad; you just have to be honorable.

Treat them with respect and you will receive it in return. If you can stay honorable and on point, they will actually protect you. Look at it from the judge's point of view, they see these idiots all day long, and NOBODY gets it! It will be a pleasure for the judge to finally have someone that is honorable in front of them.

Here are a bunch of samples to get you started:

*How can I help resolve the situation?*

*Is that required? Am I required to do that? Why?*

*Do you have any evidence that I need to be here? Is there an injured party?*

*How can I be of assistance? What can I do to help?*

*Am I required to have a license? Insurance? Registration? Permit?*

*What does that mean? What do you mean?*

*Who am I to be making any claims? Have I made any claims?*

*What does this have to do with me?*

*Would that help settle the matter?*

*Do I understand? Did I ever say I understood?*

*Who are you asking? What are you asking? Why are you                                        asking?*

*Does who understand?*

*Who is "you"? Am I a name?*

*Has there been a mistake? Would you tell me if I made a mistake?*

*Isn't the name a fiction? How could I be a name?*

*Do you want me to admit to being the name?*

*How could I be a piece of paper? Am I a piece of paper? Does paper talk?*

*Is that hearsay? Did I hear you correctly? How can I be sure? How can I answer that?*

*How may I assist the court?*

*Who is being prosecuted?*

*Who is the name? What is the name?*

*Is the name a fiction? Do I look like a fiction?*

*Who has to enter a plea?*

*Why do I have to enter a plea?*

*How am I supposed to know what to do? What would you do?*

*Why do I have to be here? Can you tell me?*

*How can I be honorable? Am I being honorable?*

*Is an answer required? How can I answer?*

*Are you a name?  Or do you have a name?*

*Why do you need me to say that name?*

*Why would I need to file or fill out paperwork?*

*Are you (the state) the injured party?*

*Can I question the state? What factually is a state? Does it even exist?*

*Are we done yet? Can I go home? Why would I sign that?*

*What does it mean to swear an oath?*

*Am I expected to know any/all of the laws? Statute? Policy? Procedure?*

*What does it mean to be charged? What is a charge?*

*How is that applicable to me?*

*Who said so? Is that true? Would you lie to me? How am I responsible?*

*How could I be responsible? How could I be of help?*

*How can I honorably settle this matter? Do you have any other questions?*

The judge probably knows the deal, but everyone else under him is bound by procedure. So you deal with the lower heads on the totem pole on their own procedure.

They must have positive ID. They will ask for your name, and you can tell them that you "believe" that you "use" the name, but you do not own it. "Can you prove I own anything?"

You don't have to answer questions (use another question), but for questions like "What is THE address?" (And not your address or my address... you don't own anything, remember?)

So this brings me to another topic about dealing with public servants, and this is when you cannot think of an appropriate question to answer with and/or you get stuck having to make a statement... ALWAYS use a non-rebuttable. Do not testify against yourself!

A non-rebuttable is a statement that rebuts a claim made, but the statement itself is non-rebuttable.

Some examples of these are; "I think...", "I believe...", "It is my opinion that...", "It appears to be..."

These are non-rebuttable because who is anyone to tell you how you think, what you believe, what your opinion is, or what things appear to you as. For instance, if you were to say something like "That car is red." That is statement is definitely rebuttable, all someone has to do is say "No, it's not red, it's crimson." But if you said "That car appears to be red.", absolutely no one will be able to rebut you.

If you EVER get past the issue of the name, you must ask the "I believe there has been a mistake; if I have I offended anyone here will you forgive me?" or "Has there been a mistake?  If I have offended anyone here can I be forgiven?"

You must not be silent. *"Silence can only be equated with fraud where there is a legal or moral duty to speak or where an inquiry left unanswered would be intentionally misleading... This sort of deception will not be tolerated and if this is the routine it should be corrected immediately."* U.S. v. Tweel, 550 F. 2d 297

Be the little child and ask the questions, and be sure to stay on point. Even if you don't do well at first, you will get better with time, practice, and experience. Keep trying, you will get it.

What about filing an affidavit or motion in your case.

I know that you would feel better filing some papers into the court, but why would you do that if once it is on paper it is hearsay, plus if you file paperwork don't you think that might be a way to ask you more questions about the tangible evidence you have filed, and even subject it to interpretation?

And then you go in to court and they ask you questions about it, and you have to answer. It isn't a good idea. Don't sign anything either.

You can swear an oath if you want, just don't make any statements, and only swear to the "statements" (which are really questions) you are to provide are truthful (but non-rebuttable).

# Conclusion

To summarize: Before you get into the questions with the judge, you need to have first declared that you are there for the matter (your response to their calling THE name), rebutted all presumptions (declared the mistake), and declared no proper notice (no contract, no meeting of the minds), and then declared your honorable intentions to help settle the matter.

THEN question, question, question, non-rebuttable statement, question, question, non-rebuttable statement, question, question, non-rebuttable statement, question, question, question, question, question till the other side drops into dishonor or the judge decides you are never going to crack and create controversy or go into dishonor. It is at this point that you will see the true reality and the court will likely zero the account whilst making up some plausible reason to dismiss the case without spooking the public gallery.

The "Peaceful Inhabitant" method may work if correctly and honorably implemented in Statutory court where they require fictional entities for their man-made fictional rules, regulations and policies to be applied to but I have a feeling that fictional representation is not required in a Superior Court of Record where Common Law is being applied with one or more independent first-hand witnesses pointing you out as the guilty party in the court room.

Be the master! Not the servant! When you go to court it will be like judge against judge, except you don't have the burden of proof so you have got it made. Just remember to practice asking questions, and staying honorable. Then when you need to you will be able to call upon your impenetrable shield of love and deflect everything that is making an attempt to harm you.

It is the inner work that makes all the difference.


GAME ON!

## ALSO BY TRENT GOODBAUDY

# YOU DON'T WANT TO READ
# WHAT THIS MAN HAS TO SAY!

### WWW.YOUDONTWANT.COM

Imagine if you could know the answers to just the important things about this life, would you spend years searching for them?

Trent's philosophy about life is unparalleled, and his views are unconventional. If your audience is looking for answers to life's toughest questions, Trent has done an excellent job of answering them and at the same time provides real, sensible advice for improving other aspects of life as well.

# THE REBIRTH OF MANKIND
# HOMO EVOLUTIS

### WWW.EVOLUTISBOOK.COM

While we were recovering from the tragedy of September 11, 2001 the global powers that be were making plans for humanity that were so large and so sweeping, they needed to keep the general public in the dark about what they were planning.

With the rapid advancement of new technology such as genetics, nanotechnology, artificial intelligence, synthetic biology, and electronics we will be able to augment and change our very bodies at the molecular level. The convergence of these technologies spell out some exciting prospects for the future, but at the same time there exists a danger so great that extinction of every living organism on the planet is closer than we think. We must be aware of our past, to know where the future leads, and we must not remain apathetic.
Ignorance is not bliss... it is terminal.
Awareness is the cure.

THESE TITLES AVAILABLE NOW AT SHOP.TRENTGOODBAUDY.COM
AND AMAZON.COM IN BOTH PAPERBACK AND KINDLE EDITIONS

## ABOUT THE AUTHOR

Trent Goodbaudy currently lives in Hillsboro, Oregon and is a professional writer, blogger, activist, photographer and web developer. Trent has a background in Aviation Maintenance Technology, Computer Science, Computer Information Systems, Programming, Design, Administrative Law, Spirituality, the true history of our planet and eventually the secrets of the Universe.

Trent is driven to write his books out of a passion for helping others, and he believes that awareness and knowing exactly who you are, and who you are **not** is the most empowering concept one can learn in life.

Made in the USA
Charleston, SC
26 December 2014